DEFYING
THE
ODDS

TRUSTED
BOOKS
A DIVISION OF DEEP RIVER BOOKS

DEFYING
THE
ODDS

STANDING UP, WHEN YOU WANT TO GIVE UP

DON WILTON

Trusted Books is an imprint of Deep River Books. The views expressed
or implied in this work are those of the author. To learn more about
Deep River Books, go online to www.DeepRiverBooks.com.

ISBN 13: 978-1-63269-340-2
Library of Congress Catalog Card Number: 2011919273

This book is dedicated to:

United States Marine 2 Lt. Andrew Kinard, committed to Christ and strong in courage. Despite losing both legs in service to our nation, Andrew is defying the odds. His growing accomplishments are matched only by his magnetic spirit and matchless resolve. Just like Noah, when the floods came, the best was yet to be!

CONTENTS

INTRODUCTION

LONG BEFORE I was born in the beautiful land of South Africa, God in His infinite knowledge designed an amazing plan for my life. Think about that! God had a specific purpose and plan for Don Wilton to be set apart, a minister of the gospel, a pastor far away in the United States of America. As a little boy growing up in the rolling hills of Zululand in Africa, the idea that God was orchestrating that plan in the circumstances of my life was simply inconceivable. Behind the scene, however, God was at work.

The odds were stacked against me from the very beginning that I would submit to God's plan for my life. I was born to wonderful parents who were successful in business, but they did not know the Lord in a deep and meaningful way. Even though they were extremely loving and caring, they did not know the deep emotional and spiritual needs of my heart as a small boy. My father was the only child of older parents who considered the echelons of boarding school superior to raising a child with a personal touch at home. Mom was my rock. They both loved me and today I cherish them beyond human gratitude. As I grew physically, my emotional and spiritual interests were left to wander aimlessly and alone. Still, the Creator of the universe was constantly at work.

The history and legacy of our family changed forever when I was six years old. That was when my father ran headlong into Jesus Christ. He went from not knowing the Lord in a deep and meaningful way to being totally secure in his relationship with the Lord, and he was determined to tell others about the gospel. Sometime later, while at boarding school, I made a decision to accept Christ into my heart and life.

We moved often and I attended five schools by the time I reached third grade. They were Christian schools, but nevertheless, they were legalistic and harsh in their methods of discipline. I walked in fear and uncertainty most of my days as a child in boarding school, and as I grew into a teenager, my heart became hardened and distant—a result of the abuses suffered there. I was far from godly during my teenage years. The Master definitely had a plan intended for my life, but the odds were not good that I would fulfill that plan. Still unknown to me, God was there, watchful and protecting.

I was drafted into the military in South Africa soon after graduating from high school. The political corruption in the country coupled with all that army life had to offer soon erupted into anger in my heart that flowed like tongues of red hot lava from Nyiragongo, a volcano north of South Africa. During my stint in the army a mound of hardened lava formed around my heart. My attitude toward life, humanity, and God was stacked against fulfilling God's appointed purpose in my life. Providentially, God continued to be at work through the prayers of my parents.

After I completed service in the military, I immediately enrolled as a freshman in university. The very next day I announced to some of my army buddies that I would attend church one Sunday morning because I knew that was where I would see the prettiest girls in town. I fell in love at first sight with the most beautiful young woman I had ever met. Karyn Bolton was her name, and she was beautiful on both the outside and inside. Her heart belonged to the Lord, and the strength she drew from Him soon drew me back into a loving relationship with Jesus Christ, showing me God was still at work in my life.

I began working through the anger in my heart as the Lord healed my hurts one by one and filled my heart with forgiveness toward those who had wounded me. Karyn and I soon married and God began to reveal His goal for our lives in ministry. Together we submitted to God's call to ministry and sold everything we owned, packed two suitcases, and with $1,400 in our pockets headed to seminary in the United States of America.

The odds that I would fulfill God's plan for my life had changed somewhat when we arrived in New York City, but they still leaned against us. We knew little about the American way of life and had few resources to help us make ends meet. But God, in His providence, provided godly people to love us and provide for our needs physically, emotionally, and spiritually. I recall countless ways He met our needs and put people into our lives to guide us. He walked beside us when we felt the pangs of hunger and He walked beside us when we had no means of transportation. He walked beside us when we did not even know how to use the air conditioner in our hand-me-down "motor car" to keep cool. God walked beside us as we drove for miles to pastor a loving church outside of New Orleans. There we lived in a small trailer with our two small sons, Rob and Greg, so we could preach the gospel each weekend.

The Father has never ceased walking beside us as we have labored in ministry among a precious people for many years. We have beaten the odds many times because we have never walked alone. There will be difficult days in our future if the

Lord tarries, but I look to Him who is the maker of heaven and earth, and I know where my help comes from—a Lord who is at work and forever will be.

I am writing this short book to encourage someone out there who is facing impossible odds. You are many and I meet you almost every day. You are me and together we can put our trust in the Lord. He has never let me down and He will not let you down. Nothing you face is too big for our God. This book is a simple testimony about the greatness of God. It is about God's goodness when the odds are against you in life. God has done for me what I cannot do for myself, and He will do the same for you. He designed a plan for Don Wilton and He has designed a plan for every other life as well, including yours. I pray that as you read *Defying the Odds* you will hold on to God because He is your hope. He is the great I Am, the Alpha and Omega, the beginning and the end. He is God Jehovah and our strength in times of need. May God bless your life and make it a testimony of His faithfulness and goodness as you beat the odds in the midst of troubled times.

CHAPTER 1

WHEN THE ODDS ARE AGAINST YOU

MY LIFE HAS not been free of struggles simply because I am a minister of the gospel. On the contrary, I remember a few summers ago when the odds were against me. I was traveling with the Mirror Image Youth Choir from my church on their summer prison tour. My left hand and arm had been feeling puffy for some time, but I simply ignored the warning signs and hoped they would go away. A motorcycle accident many years before had caused extensive injuries to my left shoulder, so I justified the puffiness as simply a result of past injuries. In addition, I surmised that an extended plane trip to my homeland in Africa could have had something to do with the puffiness. Any good excuse would do. But there was a hidden enemy looming on the horizon.

On Sunday night, after we arrived home from the youth choir tour, my arm and hand became extremely swollen to the

1

point I could not open and close my fingers. My wife would not let me ignore the warning signs any longer. She drove me to the hospital where the doctors ran tests and immediately rushed me to emergency surgery. I had a massive blood clot in my shoulder area very close to my heart. I spent several days in the intensive care unit of the hospital. It was an extremely serious situation, and for several days the doctors were deeply concerned about my prognosis.

I look back on that time and realize my life was hanging in the balance. At one point as I was waking up from surgery, I felt as if I hovered over my body with no control over what was happening to me, as if I was looking down at myself lying on the bed as the doctor pulled my wife aside, put his arm around her shoulder and said, "I am so sorry, Karyn, we have lost him." A tremendous peace came over my heart as I looked at my precious wife standing there beside my bed. This experience I cannot explain to this day, but I believe God gave me a glimpse of how I would feel should I die as a Christian man.

Soon after I came out of surgery, the doctors were very strict about my physical activity. My family tried to make me follow the doctor's orders to the letter, but realistically, my life was in God's hands and there was nothing else anyone could do. I had to depend completely on God at that point. The blood clot was a result of the constriction of blood vessels in that area—a result of injury from the motorcycle accident. I did not know it, but the odds had been stacking against me for some time.

Obviously, God spared my life, but it was the journey and not the end result that was important. I had numerous people praying for me, especially my family and church, and I believe God answered their prayers for my life and recovery. The important thing was that God had my attention! During that time of lying in the intensive care unit of the hospital, God spoke to my heart in a way He had never done before. I began to think about the scene I pictured in my mind as I was in surgery.

I began thinking about the peace I experienced at the thought of my death. Out of that situation, not only did God allow me to defy the odds, but He put into my heart a story about life after death. It was a story of two men, one a poor servant who loved Jesus and lived his life according to God's Word, and the other a rich man who lived only for money and success. They both died and embarked on a journey in opposite directions. During the next few weeks as I recovered, I wrote a novel, which I called *The Absolute Certainty of Life after Death*, which has been read by thousands of people. I would never want to go through that situation again, but it was valuable time God used to change my life and ministry. He was working all of those things together for good!

How do you face life when the odds are stacked against you? Do you keep your fingers crossed as you did when you were a child? Do you merely hope that things will get better? Do you worry, pray, or simply give up? Or do you focus completely on God and learn from your situation? Difficult situations are a fact of life. Perhaps you are in the middle of one of those situations now. Maybe you have been in a situation like that in the past and you cannot quite get over the devastation in your life. Or possibly you will face a situation like that sometime in the future. How will you handle it? Do not be discouraged. There is hope for defying the odds in your life.

I pray God will use this book in your life to encourage your heart, to cause you to be completely obedient to Him on a daily basis, and to help you rely on the power of the Holy Spirit in your life through your relationship with Jesus Christ. That relationship is best developed through reading God's Word and through prayer. There is power in prayer, but often we pray as the last resort. When we have tried everything else, and nothing works, we cry out to God for help.

Every single week we receive scores of prayer requests through our church and our broadcast ministry, "The

Encouraging Word." We are humbled to hear from every state in the United States of America and many places around the world. Think about that! People from all over the world calling because they have a need. Every Tuesday the entire ministry team of my church meets together for a time of spiritual devotion and fellowship. It is such a joy to hold written prayer requests in our hands from scores of people who have called in through our prayer lines. We read these requests and pray for each one because we believe in the power of prayer. You would be amazed to see the scope of needs among average people. The requests we receive cover every walk of life and every circumstance of life.

Why do they call "The Encouraging Word?" They call because the odds are against them. Maybe they have tried everything else, or maybe they need a miracle and they believe in prayer. They may not have the strength left in their body or mind to even voice a prayer for their need; nevertheless, they believe God listens and answers prayers. They need hope and encouragement knowing God walks through the valleys with them, and they can defy the odds with His help. The odds are against them according to the world's standards, but the Lord is working behind the scenes to bring all of those things together for good.

Are you one of those people who has a great need in life? Do not despair if you find yourself in that situation. Hold on to a glimmer of hope because of the promises in God's Word. In Joshua 1:9 God commanded Joshua, "Be strong and courageous. Do not be afraid; do not be discouraged, for the Lord your God is with you wherever you go." That same promise applies to us right where we are today. This means there is hope and comfort for our circumstances!

I received a phone call late on a Sunday evening from a young man named Chris. He called me from MD Anderson Hospital in Houston, Texas, one of the leading cancer research hospitals in the United States. Chris grew up in our church and was a friend of my two sons. Karyn and I were privileged to have him in our home often. Chris is a handsome young man who towers over most of his friends in stature. He is very talented and played varsity basketball with our two sons in high school. After Chris graduated from college, he moved to Washington, DC, and I had not seen him in seven or eight years. You can imagine how surprised I was to hear his voice.

He said, "Dr. Wilton, I needed to call and let you know what is going on with me." My heart sank as he began to relate the following story. "A couple of weeks ago I had a sore tooth that bothered me, so I went to the dentist. The dentist took a look at me and immediately referred me to an oral surgeon. They took x-rays and analyzed everything. Bottom line, Dr. Wilton, I have serious cancer in my sinus cavities. The cancer is so advanced that it has already spread to the base of my skull. I have moved from Washington, DC, to Houston, Texas for treatment. I am not allowed to go anywhere for six months. My situation is very serious. In fact, I am facing a life-threatening illness with many months of treatment and surgeries. I don't know what the outcome will be." Here is a young man only twenty-five years of age—and the odds are against him. We prayed and cried together. We continue to pray because we believe that God is working all of those things together for good in Chris's life.

We all know precious people like Chris who are going through many struggles. In a matter of a day, the fate of one family changed drastically. The husband went to work and found his company was closing and he no longer had a job. On the same day their son went to the doctor for a routine college entrance physical exam and was found to have a serious medical condition. The odds were stacked. How would they respond? Maybe you are thinking, "Pastor, I have not been diagnosed with cancer, and I have not lost my job." But every one of us will go through hard times. If you are not facing some kind of struggle right now, you either have in the past or you definitely will in the future. Because we live in a fallen world, none of us are immune to human tragedies, illnesses, and perplexities that are a part of life here on this earth. How will you respond to facing the storms of life when the odds are against you?

When I am faced with the tragedies of life, I naturally think of Job. Quite frankly, many people are no different than this servant of the Old Testament. Thousands of really wonderful people love the Lord, and try to live their lives in a way pleasing to the Lord; yet they are going through serious circumstances. I talk with people every week who are suffering with really deep issues like depression. And some are enduring terrible family struggles of different kinds. I have spoken to people who have said to me, "Pastor, please do not say anything, but my marriage is in trouble. Nobody knows about it; our children do not even know. We are in serious trouble." On occasion I counsel older couples who, though still married after many years, have become stagnant in their relationship. And to exasperate the situation, social media has sadly become a tool for some to begin new or re-establish old relationships. One or the other partner will search on the Internet and find an old classmate or sweetheart. Out of curiosity they get in touch with that person only to find themselves drawn back into their youth by sharing memories. One thing leads to another, and before they know it they have jeopardized their relationship with their lifetime spouse. They have made a grave mistake and the odds are against them.

Then there are parents who talk to me about every kind of heartache you and I can possibly imagine. Their children are angry and rebellious and are estranged from them. For many reasons, today there seem to be more and more adult children returning to their parents' homes. Some children grow up, leave home, come back home, leave, and come back home again when the going gets tough. Talk about a tough situation. How does one continue to love one's son or daughter and yet deal with the obvious complexities of having an adult "child" back in the home?

There are others who have lost loved ones: a parent, a spouse, or even a child. Death is one of the few certainties in life, but nonetheless it catches us off-guard even after much time has passed. Often I visit with precious people who have lost their soul mate of forty or fifty years, and now they feel as if all hope is gone. They are lonely, sad, and many feel that life is not worth living. When it comes to finding companionship and meaning for the rest of life, the odds are against them.

Some simply try living in obedience to God's Word, and still the odds are against them. Maybe you are ridiculed on the job simply because you live according to God's principles. Often I hear of people ostracized by co-workers or passed up for promotions simply because they are Christians. For many, the odds are against them on their jobs, in their neighborhoods, and even in their children's school. How do we overcome these struggles and defy the odds?

Perhaps you find yourself in a situation similar to one I have described, or maybe you are in a situation that is far worse. It has come to the point where you are wondering if there is any hope for survival much less in ever finding happiness and peace again. Where do you turn? What do you do next? How do you climb out of the hole you are in? Where do you go? How do you defy the odds?

All tragedies in life are difficult to deal with. Perhaps you made a mistake or were involved in some kind of sin for which you are now oppressed by guilt and blame. Maybe something happened to you and you just do not know where to turn. Perhaps you were abused as a child, or grew up in a home filled with alcoholism and anger. You reel with the results of those tumultuous years and you see the odds are against you. You have done everything you possibly can to defy the odds and now you are at the end of your rope.

In this book, I want to share ten words of encouragement from the story of Noah. Genesis 6-9 tells about the struggles of Noah. He was a righteous man who knew what it meant to have the odds against him. Picture this scenario in your mind.

Noah lived in the middle of a decidedly evil society. Indeed, his was a world without the Lord. The Bible tells us he was the only person in that society who was righteous and blameless and who found favor with God. Everyone else on the earth was evil, but Noah walked with God! One day God told Noah that He was going to destroy everyone because of their wickedness. The Lord told Noah to build a boat. Can you imagine the ridicule and taunting that Noah must have experienced in trying to be obedient to God? Here is a man building a gigantic ship in his backyard and not a drop of water in sight—let alone a lake or a sea. No wonder people must have thought he was crazy!

Not only did God tell him to build a boat, He told Noah to bring aboard the boat two of every kind of animal. Can you imagine getting instructions like that? The whole scenario was unreasonable and did not make any sense. I have never seen anybody on their hands and knees in front of a lion saying, "Here kitty, kitty, kitty. Get on my boat. We are going to have a flood!" To make matters worse, the deluge comes, and Noah and his family are stuck on an ark with thousands of animals for 150 days. No one outside the boat was spared, but God was doing something. It must have seemed as if they themselves would succumb at times, but God was at work all around Noah. Noah simply had to trust God, be obedient, and let Him work.

Genesis 6:5 reads, "The Lord saw how great man's wickedness on the earth had become....The Lord was grieved that he had made man on the earth, and his heart was filled with pain." That is an interesting statement about the character of God. His heart was filled with pain. But Noah found favor in the eyes of God. He was a righteous man, blameless among the people of his time. And Noah walked with God. He did all God commanded.

He made himself an ark of cypress wood, with rooms coated and pitched inside and out. God said to him, "Noah, I will establish my covenant with you and you will enter the ark. You and your sons, your wife and sons' wives with you." This unimaginable disaster is reported in God's Word as we read that, "every living thing on the face of the earth was wiped out from the earth."

In the middle of this entire trauma here comes Noah. Talk about defying the odds! Talk about a new "Survivor" series! After some time God caused a wind to blow over the earth and the waters receded.

The first thing God's servant did when he stepped back onto dry land was to build an altar. Then God blessed him. What a sweet word that is...*blessed*! "Then God blessed Noah and his sons saying to them, "Be fruitful and multiply in number and fill the earth. The fear and dread of you will fall on all of the beasts of the earth and all of the birds of the air, upon every creature that moves along the ground and upon all the fish of the sea; they are given into your hands. Everything that lives and moves will be food for you. Just as I gave you green plants, I now give you everything.'"

On occasion hurting people can be heard making statements similar to some of these: "I have lost it all." "My life will never be the same again." "I am going down the drain." "My life is over." "I can never recoup what I have lost." "I can never find wholeness and meaning in my life again." "I think God has abandoned me." And the most serious of all, "I am just going to end it all!" I want you to know the Lord Jesus has not abandoned you. With God's help you can stand up again. You can recover. You can be made whole.

You may be thinking, *How can that happen when the odds are against me?* Noah beat the odds because he completely trusted God. God warned him of an impending storm and Noah heeded the warning signs. God told him to build an ark and he did. God gave him specific instructions and Noah followed those instructions exactly, even when they did not make any sense to him. Had this early shipbuilder known the words to one of our favorite hymns, "Trust and obey, for there's no other way to be happy in Jesus, but to trust and obey," he might have led his entire family in a special rendition of that song from the bow of the ark.

In the following chapters I will share ten words of encouragement drawn from the biblical narrative. I am praying for every person who picks up this book because God's Word "never returns void." This means God has placed His guarantee of blessing on His Word, and, as such, your specific situation and circumstance will be dealt with regardless of whether or not I have mentioned it. Jesus Christ has an encouraging word just for you!

At the end of each chapter there are questions to think about and answer. This is not a test, but simply a way to help you process what you have read. Stop and ask God to work in your mind and heart today as you read the questions and think about your life. I pray you will feel His presence in a mighty way as you meditate upon His Word.

STUDY QUESTIONS

Are you facing a crisis or struggle in your life right now? Describe it below. If not, write about a struggle you faced in the past.

_____

_____

_____

_____

Read the story of Noah in Genesis 6-9, and list the odds against Noah.

_____

_____

_____

_____

What are the odds against you right now?

_____

_____

_____

_____

Noah beat the odds against him by trusting God completely and being obedient in every way. How do you trust God in your situation?

_____

_____

_____

_____

How can you be obedient to God's Word in your situation?

_____

_____

_____

_____

Write a prayer below asking God to help you trust Him and to be completely obedient to His Word.

_____

_____

_____

_____

GOD SEES

The Lord saw how great man's wickedness on the earth had become, and that every inclination of the thoughts of his heart was only evil all the time....But Noah found favor in the eyes of the Lord.

—Gen. 6:5, 8

IN 2010, KARYN and I became empty nesters, and the situation has been bittersweet. The children gave us so much joy and we thoroughly enjoyed rearing them, but the time came for them to leave the nest and soar. God blessed us with two wonderful sons in a matter of two years, and nine years later gave us our precious little princess, whom I affectionately call "Tweety." Shelley has always been a "Daddy's girl" and we both love one another's attention. Like most small children, "Watch me, Daddy" seemed to be one of her favorite expressions growing up.

The onset of college invariably was accompanied by hours of joyful recollection of sun-filled memories. You know those days when you go down to the beach for a week of vacation. You get out the umbrella, chairs, shovels, buckets, sun block, towels, snacks, and all of the other important paraphernalia you need when you have young children. You plant your chair and umbrella on the sand while the children run around happily occupied in every way. With buckets in hand they dig for digging's sake alone and walk back and forth carrying endless loads of seawater to holes that never seem to co-operate and fill up! "Watch me, Daddy! Watch me, Daddy! Watch me, Mommy!"

As loving parents we watch because we love our children. They are the most important people on this earth, and we care deeply about them and their welfare. When our child heads in a direction that could cause them injury or danger, we step in to save the day. We are watching when they disobey the rules, and we watch when they are being obedient, ready to discipline or reward accordingly.

Before you know it, your children have grown up. They become teenagers and begin to play sports, sing, or play a musical instrument. And they still want mom and dad to watch. A child never gets past that stage when you really think about it. There is an innate desire for mom and dad to watch and be proud. Even as adults, we want our parents to be at important events in our lives. Even now, after Dad has listened to me preach, I appreciate his words of encouragement. My parents are proud of me and that blesses my heart. There is something deeply important in the hearts of parents to see firsthand what is going on their child's life.

So it is with our Heavenly Father. The first word of encouragement in our study is that "God sees." God is always watching. You are not alone, and you have not been abandoned. He is watching and He sees. He is watching because He loves you and because you are important to Him. He is watching because He cares. He is watching to discipline and to reward. He created you for a purpose.

In Noah's day, God was totally cognizant of the evil of mankind. He saw what was happening on the earth. God saw not only the evil, but He saw Noah's heart and thoughts, and his walk and talk as well. The Father saw Noah was trustworthy and obedient. He needed someone to carry on His creation, someone upon whom He could trust and depend. He had been watching over Noah's life and actions, and God chose Noah to carry out His kingdom plan.

If you really think about it, Noah probably struggled deep in his heart with that plan. Can you imagine the public ridicule he must have endured? At times, maybe doubt even crept into his mind and heart. But Noah was trustworthy and obedient, and he never gave up.

But what if Noah had given up? What if he said, "Forget this! I am tired of people laughing at me for building a boat. It is never going to rain. It has not so far! Why should it now?" What would have been the outcome if Noah had disobeyed God? Would God have chosen another person to carry on his creation? Or would that have been the end to the human race as we know it? We will never have the answer to those questions this side of heaven, but they are important questions to consider as we battle with our struggles in life.

Does God have a bigger plan than what you and I see? Yes, absolutely. Does He desire to use our struggles in His Kingdom plan? Again, absolutely. If I give up and do not trust and obey Him, will He use another person? Possibly! Proverbs 19:21 teaches, "Many are the plans in a person's heart, but it is the Lord's purpose that prevails." Will I miss out on the blessings and rewards if I do not endure to the end? There is no doubt about that. Obedience is the hallmark of Christian discipleship. It is really the foundation of faith—it is the way of salvation.

Without full obedience it is impossible to please God. Absolute obedience produces the blessings of the Lord. This is so clearly seen in the life of Noah.

I love the words of that beautiful song, "His Eye is on the Sparrow and I know He watches me." This is an incredibly profound statement. Think about it. When we find ourselves in the most perplexing circumstances of life, God is watching over us. There in the hospital bed where you have just received a terminal diagnosis, God sees what is going on. When you go home and it is like stepping into a war zone, God does not turn away. When sons and daughters disappoint us, God sees. When we struggle financially, or when we are in the pit of depression, God sees. He sees when a world without Christ demonstrates against us. Even when circumstances do not make sense, God sees. The Father is watching and He knows every inclination of the thoughts of our hearts.

In whatever circumstance you find yourself today, God sees in the midst of life's struggles! He cares about you and your welfare. He is watching and He is proud when you walk with Him despite your circumstances. Take time to thank Him right now because He never takes His eyes off of you.

STUDY QUESTIONS

When God looks down at your life, what do you think He sees? What are the inclinations of your heart toward your situation right now?

_____

_____

_____

_____

At this point, do you think God finds you trustworthy and obedient?

_____

_____

_____

_____

If not, what do you need to change in order to be trustworthy and obedient to God?

_____

_____

_____

_____

Often it is easy to make it through a struggle by looking back and remembering God's faithfulness in the past. Think about a time in your life when you went through a crisis or struggle. How do you know that God saw your struggle?

_____

_____

_____

_____

Can you look back now and see how God was working all around you during the struggle, even though you did not know it at the time? How did God use your crisis or struggle to advance His Kingdom plan?

_____

_____

_____

_____

Write a prayer of thanksgiving to God because He is watching over you. Tell Him how you feel about your life right now.

_____

_____

_____

_____

CHAPTER 3

GOD GRIEVES

The Lord was grieved that He had made man on the earth, and His heart was filled with pain.

—Gen. 6:6

PARENTS GRIEVE WHEN their children are sick, mistreated, or in pain. When a child hurts, the parent hurts as much or more. Most parents love their children and want the very best for them. They do not want to see their children suffer because they have a deep connection in their hearts. All my married life I have seen the pain in my wife's parents' hearts on the anniversary of the death of their oldest daughter. Priscilla was very precious to them and always will be. Few things in life must hurt more than the loss of a child. Mickey and Debbie Sobeski will attest to this fact. The following is Hannah's story in her daddy's words:

Hannah Marie Sobeski was an All-American girl who loved life and lived it to its fullest. She would be the first to tell you that she was simply a sinner saved by grace. Hannah loved her Lord and Savior, Jesus Christ, and faithfully served Him in all she did. In May of 2006, near the end of her junior year of high school, Hannah learned that she had a rare form of Sarcoma cancer. The tumor was growing rapidly and required immediate treatment. She spent seventy-seven days at the MD Anderson Cancer Center in Houston, Texas, undergoing aggressive chemotherapy. During this time, Hannah's story of faith and praise in the midst of her storm captivated her entire community. It has since spread all across America and into many foreign countries. God did many miraculous things through Hannah's life and journey. Perhaps none was greater than sustaining her for thirty days in ICU on a ventilator, then restoring her strength to the point she came home to Spartanburg, South Carolina, to continue her treatment. As friends and classmates went busily along with their senior year of high school, Hannah was in and out of the hospital. God had a final big moment planned for Hannah as her classmates nominated her for the Homecoming court. She was voted as the 2006 Dorman High School Homecoming Queen by the student body. On a chilly night in October, she was crowned queen to thunderous applause. The next day she learned that her tumor had doubled in size and without a miraculous healing from God, her time left here was short. Hannah believed until her last breath on earth and her first in heaven that God was going to heal her. On November 9, 2006, in the presence of her family and a home filled with friends, He did. He healed her wholly and completely, as our Homecoming Queen went home to eternity to be with her King! (© 2006-2008 Hannah's Hope Ministries, used by permission.)

Mickey and Debbie know Hannah is with the Lord Jesus Christ in heaven, and they have a significant ministry as a result of Hannah's life and death. But they still grieve because of their loss. In addition to Hannah, I have preached at the funerals of two other teenage girls who were very active in our church in the last three years. Bethany lost her life to leukemia, and Brittany's life was taken instantly in a car accident. To this day, even though the parents of those girls all have great faith in God, they are still grieving in their own way. One mother said, "It has been over three years and I still cannot bear to look at pictures or home videos. It is still too painful."

Most parents do not dare even to think about the possibility of being separated from their child through death. Losing a child in a tragic accident, to cancer, or other illness is devastating no matter how old the son or daughter is. But, as a pastor, I want to say it is equally as devastating to lose a child to sin. I have had the unenviable duty of counseling parents who have lost a child not to death but to sinful choices. Some have lost a child to drugs and alcohol, or illicit relationships. Others have lost a child who has run away, or some have been separated from their son or daughter because they are in juvenile detention centers or prison. Nothing grieves the heart of a parent worse than being separated from their child whether it is a result of death or sinful choices. And so it is with our Heavenly Father.

Have you ever thought about the heart of God, His grief over our sins and His pain when we are hurt? Oddly enough, the second word of encouragement is that "God grieves." You may think, *How can this be a word of encouragement?* Deep grief can only be experienced when there is deep love. Have you thought about His longing to be with His children when they are separated from Him because of sin? We see this clearly in Genesis 6:6. In this context God "grieves" in the sense that He is "righteously angered" by man's sin. He grieves because of the separation caused by sin, but His grieving speaks to the longing of His heart for man to be reconciled to Him. It is right here, in this powerful book of origins, that God vividly portrays His grieving heart. There are three ways God grieves:

GOD GRIEVES WITH US

God is our Heavenly Father and He has a deep heart connection with us. This truth ought to be embedded deep in our hearts. Jesus Christ became man, came to this earth, and identified with us in all things, except that He did not sin. In His flesh He identified with our pain. Through the sacrifice of the Son, we now have a High Priest who, as God, grieves with us. This is where we see the empathetic nature of a Creator who loves us, who grieves right there alongside us. When we hurt, He hurts. When we are abused, He feels the pain. When we are sick and suffering, God suffers with us. When we grieve, He grieves along with us.

GOD GRIEVES FOR US

God not only unites himself with us and shares in our grief, but He hovers over us as the God of heaven and, in His sovereign grace, He grieves for us when we do not even understand that we should be grieving. We may be ignorant of our circumstances. But God sees and He knows when to grieve for us. This can be compared to a parent who sees their child making wrong decisions. Symbolically, perhaps, they see a son or daughter going the wrong way down a one-way street. They know the outcome is not going to be good. They try to guide their child, but the child ignores the direction. The child is stubborn and thinks he or she is making the right decisions. But loving and caring parents know better. The son and daughter have no idea they should be grieving over their life's destination. They have no idea they are destroying their lives. They could have everything, but they are headed for nothing. The parent grieves in the same way God grieves for us. He has a perfect plan for our lives. He wants to give us the best, but often we stray off the path God has planned for us. And God grieves for us.

GOD GRIEVES BECAUSE OF US

In a different way, because He is a righteous and holy God, the Father grieves because of our willful sin. Genesis 6:6 essentially portrays God in this light. He was grieved in His heart over the sins of humankind. He was sorry He had made man. God grieves when we do not live for Him. He grieves when we willfully go against His Word and live a life of blatant rebellion. God grieves because we bear in our bodies the consequences of the sinful people we are.

Grief is expressed when the heart is broken, and great grief is a result of great love! Could it be possible that God's heart is broken for you today?

- Are you grieving because of your circumstances in life? If so, take great comfort knowing God is grieving with you. He is right there beside you.
- Is it possible you are headed down a path toward destruction? Could it be possible that God is grieving for you and you do not even realize there is a reason for grief?
- Or could it be that God grieves because of you? Do you have willful, intentional sin in your life but are too prideful to open your heart in repentance?

Examine your life today and respond to God's broken heart for your life. Whatever your circumstance today, God is right there with you. Allow Him to put His loving arms around you today and draw you close to Him.

STUDY QUESTIONS

Read 1 Peter 1:3-8. Are you grieving because of some circumstance in your life today? What can you learn from these verses
that will help you?

_____

_____

_____

_____

Does God have reason to grieve for you today? Write a prayer
below asking the Holy Spirit to convict your heart of any
unknown sin in your life.

_____

_____

_____

_____

Are you willfully sinning in your life at this time? Is there a secret
room in your heart that no one knows about but you? If so, God
is grieving because of you today. Read the following verses and
write your response to God:

a) Job 42:1-6

_____

_____

_____

_____

b) Jeremiah 17:9

_____

_____

_____

_____

c) Matthew 4:17

_____

_____

_____

_____

d) Acts 26:20

_____

_____

_____

_____

Write a prayer thanking God for His great love for you.

_____

_____

_____

_____

GOD KNOWS

But Noah found favor in the eyes of the Lord. This is the
account of Noah. Noah was a righteous man, blameless
among the people of his time, and he walked with God.
—Gen. 6:8-9

WHEN I WAS sixteen years old, I went to my parents and
announced I was leaving home for a good while to embark on
a journey into the wild of Africa—a safari of sorts. My best
friend made the same proclamation to his family, and the two
of us loaded our backpacks and off we went to conquer the vast
bush lands of the continent. South Africa is composed of three
geographically diverse regions. There is an expansive central
plateau, a massive continuous mountain range surrounding the
plateau, and a strip of low-lying, but mountainous, land along
the coast. South Africa is one of the most beautiful areas you

will ever see. There are lush forests, the splendor of towering waterfalls, and amazing wildlife. South Africa has it all.

One of the most chilling events of our trip happened one evening at dusk while watching one of the most incredible sunsets we had ever witnessed. I remember leaning against a tree entranced as the orange ball slid beneath the horizon. It was as though I was watching a promotional video for a fabulous African safari vacation, with sound effects included. In the near distance, we heard the most distinct, bone-chilling sound that young men in the bush can hear. It was nothing other than the sound of a hungry lion roaring his order for dinner. Our inspiring moment watching the sunset came to an abrupt end as we snapped into action, and before you knew it, we had a roaring blaze going that would light up half of Africa. We came as close to sleeping in the fire as one could get, and at the first sign of sunrise we intrepid adventurers headed home.

In thinking back over that situation, I started to understand a few things about that lion. First of all, I knew his nature. I knew his capabilities and his lack of inhibitions. I knew what lions liked to eat and I knew what time of day they enjoyed their meal. I knew lions would not come close to fire, so I built a big one. I knew about the lion, but I did not want to know him personally.

The third word of encouragement is that "God knows." He knows you down to the core of your being and He wants you to know Him as well. Many people today know about God and many love Him in a very real way. But many spend such a little time with Him in prayer, worship, and the study of His Word, that they do not "get to know Him" in a real personal way. He has a desire to relate to you one on one. He made you for his pleasure, and He has a deep desire to have an intimate relationship with every person.

And so it was in the days of Noah. Of all of the people on the earth, the masses of society, God knew each one of them to their very core. Noah was one tiny person sprinkled among the thousands of people on the earth. He was merely a drop in the bucket, as it were, but God knew him down to the depths of his heart, and Noah found favor in the eyes of the Lord.

Pain and struggles can cause us to arrive at a point where we actually believe we have been forgotten by God. We often think, *How could the God of the universe want to have a relationship with me?* That is particularly true in the lives of people who have gone through years of struggle. We know people just like us who have endured struggles in their lives, people who have been faithful and who relentlessly tried everything that can be imagined, but the struggle never seems to go away. It never seems to get to the point in which they can get back on their feet. The pain is always there.

Sin still remains the greatest source of pain in the believer's life. Nothing is good about it. And there is no such thing as "soft" sin. According to God's Word, sin is sin, and it separates us from God. Because He is righteous and holy, God cannot accommodate, tolerate, or tiptoe around sin in any form or fashion. Because sin separates us, it is sometimes natural to think God has forgotten us when we have sin in our life. But God still longs for a relationship with us especially in the midst of sin. This is why Christians are invited to "confess their sin." In so doing they discover "Jesus is faithful and just to forgive our sin and cleanse us from all unrighteousness." He knows what is going on in your life and is grieved by it.

Maybe you were once close to God and had a growing relationship with Him, but now you feel a distance. My question is, "Who has strayed away?" That age-old caption, "Does God seem farther away? Well, who do you think moved?" still hits the nail on the head! God longs to be close to you. He knows your circumstances and He stands waiting for you to come back to Him.

Just a quick word about the impact of both cause and effect on a person's life. When you have suffered great loss, but you allow God to do what only God can do and you hand it over to Him, you will always remember the event, but the pain will lessen as you allow God to heal your hurts. He bears our burdens for us. It is not unlike Jesus' instruction, in The Lord's Prayer, to forgive others. When we forgive others, even when we have been deeply hurt, we may still recall the reason why we were hurt or offended—but without the pain that accompanies it. Often we think, *I am just going to be a wonderful Christian and hand it all over to God*, then comes tomorrow and the whole thing comes back to the table again. I have never read in the Bible that God takes over one's circumstances and erases entire events from one's memory. And, perhaps there are times when it is best for us to remember the pain. When we have sinned grievously and remember the pain we caused, we will be less likely to repeat that sin. It is like a child who touches a hot stove. She remembers the pain and that pain prevents her from touching the stove again. It could be the sin of another person that has caused you pain. That person's sin can also prevent you from making the same mistake. When you see the pain and heartache in the other person's life, it will be easier to avoid the sin they have committed.

Things will happen in our lives, often through no fault of our own, and we will always remember them. But, mercifully, we can remember it with less pain as time goes by. The Bible says Noah found favor in the eyes of God. He was the only person on earth who lived a righteous life, and still Noah had to go through the storm. Why did God not choose another way to destroy evil on the earth? Why did he choose for Noah to ride out the storm with his family on a boat with thousands of animals for 150 days?

When we go through the storms of life, we gaze at God. We develop character to live life in a way that is pleasing to God and helpful to others. While no one wishes pain on another, there is no doubt that those who have walked through the trials of life seem to have a far greater empathy than most. Some of the greatest "comforters" are people who really know what it means to be "comforted." If you have never experienced pain, heartache, or great loss, you can never truly understand what it feels like to be heartbroken. We must go through the storm and keep our eyes fixed on our Lord Jesus Christ. He will show us the rainbow at the end of the storm.

Often people ask God, "Why did you allow this to happen to me?" "What have I done to deserve this?" "Why do You allow bad things to happen to good people?" We probably will not know the answers to those questions this side of heaven, but we can be assured that God knows our pain, suffering, heart, and motives. He knows all of our names, and exactly how many hairs are on every head. He knows every detail of your life and He wants to know you in a deep and intimate way. You may feel that you are only one tiny person sprinkled among the masses of society, but God knows you down to the core of your being. He is working around you, in you, and through you. To borrow a beautiful little song we sing with children, "He's still working on me, to make me what I ought to be!" Open your heart to Him. If you have never asked Christ to come into your heart and life, do it today.

STUDY QUESTIONS

Think about a time in your life when you thought God had forgotten you. Discuss how you felt during that time.

_____

_____

_____

_____

How do you think Noah might have felt on day 100 during the flood? Write what you think could have possibly happened on the ark during the 150 days.

_____

_____

_____

_____

God knows every detail of your life. He knows you to the core of your heart. What do you need to say to God about the condition of your heart today?

_____

_____

_____

_____

Write a prayer thanking God for caring about the details of your life.

_____

_____

_____

_____

If you have never invited Jesus into your heart, write a prayer asking Him to enter your life today.

_____

_____

_____

_____

CHAPTER 5

GOD DIRECTS

So God said to Noah, "I am going to put an end to all people, for the earth is filled with violence because of them. I am surely going to destroy both them and the earth.

So make yourself an ark of cypress wood; make rooms in it and coat it with pitch inside and out. This is how you are to build it: The ark is to be 450 feet long, 75 feet wide and 45 feet high. Make a roof for it and finish the ark to within 18 inches of the top. Put a door in the side of the ark and make lower, middle, and upper decks.

I am going to bring floodwaters on the earth to destroy all life under the heavens, every creature that has the breath of life in it. Everything on earth will perish. But I will establish my covenant with you, and you will enter the ark—you and your sons and your wife and your sons' wives with you.

You are to bring into the ark two of all living creatures, male and female, to keep them alive with you. Two of every kind of bird, of every kind of animal and every kind of creature that moves along the ground will come to you to be kept alive. You are to take every kind of food that is to be eaten and store it away as food for you and for them."

Noah did everything just as God commanded him.

—Gen. 6:13-22

I LOVE NEW Orleans! I love the food, the people, the area, the beignets, and the coffee. I attended the New Orleans Baptist Theological Seminary and after I graduated, I was privileged to be the Associate Professor of Evangelistic Preaching at the seminary for a number of years. My children were born there, and my wife and I spent many good years in the Big Easy. Both of my sons graduated from the seminary and live in New Orleans, and all five of my grandsons, so far, have been born there as well. Consequently, you can imagine how I felt on hearing that Hurricane Katrina was headed for New Orleans. It was not just any hurricane, but a major category five hurricane.

I was at a retreat center in Pass Christian, Louisiana, when the storm warnings came. I was privileged to be part of a group of men from the seminary who met to pray for New Orleans. We prayed on Friday night well into the night. Then the students got into their cars and headed back to the seminary in the middle of the night to get their families and evacuate. I flew out the next morning from Mobile, Alabama, just in time to avoid the devastation.

The retreat center where we prayed was completely destroyed only hours after I left. A few years after the devastation I was in the area and drove out to see what lasting damage the retreat center had suffered, and if they had repaired the damages in the years since. Behind a fence with overgrown weeds, what was left of the retreat center looked like a bombed-out building in a war torn country. Chills ran up my spine as I wondered what would have been the result had I ignored the warning and decided to ride out the storm. Only God knows the answer to that question, but I can only imagine that I would not be here today.

There were hurricane warnings all along the Gulf Coast and in the city of New Orleans. Radar was used to track the course of the storm as it headed straight for the Big Easy. Experts knew the levies were weak, and with a storm of this magnitude they could easily break. People were given specific instructions to evacuate, but many, for whatever reason, ignored the warnings and chose not to leave. Some had no transportation, and others did not want to leave their homes unattended. Many simply were not physically able to leave. Others did not believe the hurricane would harm them. Sadly, nearly 2,000 deaths have been attributed to Hurricane Katrina.

What if Noah had ignored God's storm warning? It is an amazing thing to consider the exactness of God's instructions in warning Noah of the impending flood. Noah had never seen an ark before. He certainly had no idea what flood waters could do. Noah had probably never seen rain before, much less a flood. He would have been helpless to save himself or his family. Without God's direction, they would have perished along with the others.

Noah Knew God's Voice

The fourth word of encouragement is that "God directs." It is a comfort and a blessing to know God gives us specific directions in our lives. We can learn more about obeying God's directions by studying the life of Noah. Why did Noah obey God and not some other person on the earth? Why was he willing to take such a risk? None of it made any sense. Yet, Noah was willing to risk it all because he knew God's voice. Genesis 6:9 records that, "Noah walked with God." Repeated and consistent fellowship with God always produces friendship with God. Real friends get to know one another intimately. It is evident Noah had a long and growing relationship with God. He knew God well enough to recognize the divine voice when God spoke to him.

Growing up in South Africa, I worked on a sheep farm, one of the many jobs I had as a young man. One thing I learned in working with sheep is that they know the shepherd's voice. They knew who fed them and who took care of them. When the shepherd spoke, the sheep followed because they recognized his voice. In the same way, Noah recognized God's voice because he walked with Him.

NOAH LISTENED TO GOD'S VOICE

When God spoke, Noah recognized His voice and listened. He knew who sustained him, and who took care of him. When God spoke, Noah was eager to hear what He had to say. Just as the sheep came when the shepherd spoke, Noah listened when God spoke. The sheep knew the shepherd had food, but Noah knew God had something more important than food.

NOAH OBEYED GOD'S DIRECTIONS

If Noah had been neglectful of God's specific instructions, he could have perished as well. Suppose Noah had thought, *Oh, I do not really see the need to coat this ark with pitch. It is pretty messy and I really do not want to go to all that trouble.* The results would have been disastrous.

Did you know that God loves you so much that He takes care of the finest, most intricate, smallest details of your life? Consider a man who is going to have heart surgery. He has a heart condition and the doctors have told him he needs to have heart surgery in order to save his life. As the cardiologist and team of medical personnel are standing around the table, how is the patient to pray? How should family and friends of the patient pray? As young people we used to sing a chorus that carried such profound significance in terms of God's sovereign power. The words went something like this: "God is so great, He rules this mighty universe. And yet He is so small, He lives within my heart!" Wow! This song really says it all. The answer is that we can pray about the very smallest intricate details of our lives in addition to praying about all the catastrophic things that are plain for everyone to see.

Nothing about us lies outside the scope of God's touch. We read in the Old Testament that man is fearfully and wonderfully made. Did you know God literally knit us together in the smallest detail? He knows everything. He directs each neuron that fires in our brains and numbers every hair on our heads. He directs in detail. He understands every spark plug in the body, every nerve fiber. When God told Noah to build an ark, He did not just say, "Get out there and start building. You have a bunch of sons, so build a boat." Instead, He gave Noah very specific instructions. God directs in an incredible way. Not only did God direct Noah's life, but He will do the same for you. When you know His voice, listen to His directions, and are completely obedient to Him, then you will be in the center of God's will, and that is the most satisfying place to be on this earth.

DIRECTIONS FROM GOD

How does God speak to us today? Do we hear Him audibly? Is there a roaring boom from Heaven? Today our directions from God come in several ways. Most often, God uses the Bible to direct us. He gave us His Word as the guidebook for our lives. As God's "lamp" and "light" the Bible enables us to see ahead when we, otherwise, cannot see. When trying to make a decision or seek guidance in a particular situation, it is important to ask, "What does God's Word say about this situation?" If your decision does not line up with the principles in the Bible, you can certainly know God is not leading you in that direction.

At other times, God speaks clearly through our circumstances. For example, if you are trying to make a decision concerning a job, God may close the door and you have no decision to make. When God closes one door, He may open a door in a direction you have never dreamed possible. At other times, God will direct through prayer by speaking to one's heart while praying. A thought will come into the mind seemingly out of thin air. If that thought lines up with God's Word, God may be directing through his Holy Spirit. Other times, God speaks to us through other people. In my own experience it would take another book to record the numbers of godly people who have been used of the Lord to help guide me when I needed to defy the odds for God.

But the litmus test always goes back to His Word. If you think God is directing you to do a certain thing, it is amazing just how often He lines everything up with His Word. This is why having a regular time with the Lord is so vital. Our ministry sends out thousands of devotionals called "The Daily Encouraging Word Bible Guide." I cannot tell you the numbers of calls, e-mails, and messages we have received from people all across the nation who bear testimony to God's guidance and the reading of His Word. When you begin every day with a time of prayer and the reading of a passage from God's Word, you position yourself to hear from the Lord. This is just one of the many reasons I encourage you to meet with the Lord in prayer and with a daily reading every day.

Often God gives warnings in life so we can avoid unnecessary storms. Sometimes there are no warnings, and God leads us through the storm. He will use every storm in life to bring you closer to Him and mold you into the person He wants you to be. Remember He is the potter and we are the clay. When going through the storms of life and holding onto God's hand, listen to His voice, and obey His every direction, He will use your life for His Kingdom purpose.

STUDY QUESTIONS

When we go through the storms of life, it is often difficult to see the warnings that came before the storm. Can you look back on a storm you have weathered and see the warnings that came before the storm? What were those warnings?

_____

_____

_____

_____

What could you have done differently, if anything?

_____

_____

_____

_____

Are you going through a specific situation now in your life? If so, get alone in a quiet place and ask God to speak to you. Ask Him for specific instructions. Write what He reveals to you below. When you finish writing, make sure that what you have written measures up to God's Word.

_____

_____

_____

_____

Has God given you instructions for a specific situation? What do you need to do today to be obedient to His instructions?

_____

_____

_____

_____

Write a prayer to God. Tell Him about the details of your situation and ask Him to show you what to do.

_____

_____

_____

_____

Ask God to show you how He wants to use the storms of your life for His kingdom purpose. Listen to his directions, write them below, and begin to live your life accordingly.

_____

_____

_____

_____

CHAPTER 6

GOD ESTABLISHES

But I will establish my covenant with you, and you will enter the ark with your sons, your wife, and your sons' wives.

—Gen. 6:18

I confirm my covenant with you that never again will all flesh be wiped out by the waters of a deluge; there will never again be a deluge to destroy the earth. And God said, "This is the sign of the covenant I am making between Me and you and every living creature with you, a covenant for all future generations: I have placed My bow in the clouds, and it will be a sign of the covenant between Me and the earth."

—Gen. 9:11-13 HCSB

A COVENANT IS an agreement between God and people. God is the initiating party in the covenant. As the initiator, He is the governing authority. Covenants usually include certain conditions that must be followed in order for benefits to be granted. Throughout Scripture God affirms His formula for success in the Christian life. Obey and be blessed—disobey and be cursed! In Genesis, God established his covenant with Noah before the flood, just as He would later with Abraham. It is significant to note that the word "establish" is written in future tense. In Genesis 6:18 God established his covenant with Noah before he boarded the boat, but Scripture does not indicate that God told Noah exactly what the covenant was until after the flood. There is a direct correlation between what God is doing for you today and what He will do for you tomorrow. There is a connection that is inherent in the establishment of the covenant of God between the heart of man, the heart of God, and the lifetime of man. From that moment on, God not only established His covenant with Noah, but with mankind. The fifth word of encouragement is that "God establishes." In other words, at that time, God spoke about His divine purpose for every person.

A young couple in my congregation named Derek and Ginger Parks prayed faithfully for God to give them a baby. They soon found they were expecting identical twin boys. A couple of months into the pregnancy, the doctor informed them the babies had twin-to-twin transfusion, meaning one twin was receiving all of the nourishment, blood, and fluids, while the other twin was not receiving enough to thrive. The donor twin was very small and the other twin was much larger. The doctor gave the couple the devastating news that the donor twin would become sicker as the days continued and would more than likely die, and could possibly even cause the other twin to die as well. The doctor advised selective abortion where he would abort the small twin and allow the other baby to live. This young couple left the doctor's office, went to their car, and cried out to God. They named their boys, Kade and Kyle, and trusted Him to bring both babies through.

According to the world, the odds were stacked against the Parks if they did not choose abortion. Because of their strong convictions on the sanctity of life, and their trust in a sovereign God, they never considered abortion for a second. They obeyed God and vowed to allow Him to give or take away as He saw fit.

The days ahead were dark at times and the pregnancy was hard. This young mother-to-be spent many days in the hospital where the doctors monitored her blood flow to the babies. One morning, two-and-a-half months early, the doctor informed them that they had to perform an emergency C-section in order to save both babies. With separate teams of doctors and nurses for each baby, they were delivered and rushed to the neonatal intensive care unit where they stayed for ninety days.

Kyle weighed two pounds and Kade weighed three. It was touch and go for weeks, and then the weeks turned into months. Both babies had serious problems because their lungs were not fully developed, and their kidneys were not functioning properly at times. The parents were not allowed to hold their babies for many weeks. Both babies were in incubators and on respirators, IVs, and oxygen. They were hooked up to monitors that beeped every time they stopped breathing, or if their heart rate was too slow or fast, or if their oxygen level was too low. To stack the odds even further against the babies, Kyle contracted a serious staph infection and Kade had an infection in his leg where the IV was connected. They were both on strong antibiotics and multiple other medicines. The days were dark and depressing. The odds were against them and at times it seemed they would not make it.

Only the parents and grandparents were permitted in the NICU and many times in the middle of the night, they would wake up and not be able to sleep. They would dress, go to the hospital, and sit in the NICU praying for God to bring the babies through. After ninety long days, both babies were well enough to come home.

Today, Derek and Ginger have two very fine boys and a precious big sister, Kendall, too! The little boys are healthy with no long-term effects from the early lung and kidney problems. God asked for obedience, and this young couple obeyed. They went through the storm, but today they see the rainbow every time those little boys look into their eyes and say, "I love you more, Mommy!" "I love you more, Daddy!" God put his stamp on this young couple, and He has a divine purpose for Kyle and Kade. I look forward to seeing how God will use these young men as they grow up.

God established His covenant by putting the rainbow in the sky as a reminder that He will never again destroy all flesh on the earth by a flood. Genesis 9:12-13 reminds us that this is a covenant for future generations as well. Every time you see a rainbow, it is a reminder that God established His covenant with Noah and with you. He had a plan and a divine purpose for Noah, just as He does for you.

But Noah had to go through the storm. God had a plan and purpose for his life—a specific job for Noah to do. When Noah's family embarked on the ark and the rain started, they had no choice. But God was with them every moment. All living things on the earth were destroyed. Noah beat the odds because God had a plan. He beat the odds because he obeyed God to the minutest detail and because he trusted God to take care of him. God established His covenant with Noah to show His plan and protection for the pinnacle of His creation. God put His stamp on Noah and he was never the same again. When we go through the storms of life, in essence, God is putting His stamp on us. We will never be the same again.

I am sure there were days when Noah felt unsure and afraid. He had never seen it rain that way before, and possibly he felt a little seasick at times, but he never gave up. Maybe he was fed up with cleaning up after all those animals day after day, but he never gave up. Maybe he wondered if this was to be his lot in life from now on, but he never gave up. He continued to trust

God, because God had established His covenant with Noah before he got on the boat.

Are you in the middle of a great storm in your life? Do the odds seem stacked against you and things are not looking good? Remember that God loves you. He has a purpose and plan for your life. When you get through the storm, you will never be the same. Just as Noah was, you can be wiser, more experienced, more dependent on God, and much more useful for His kingdom than you were before the storm. Trust Him during the storms of life. Continue to look up to Him no matter what your circumstances, and in the end He will show you the rainbow that comes at the end of the storm.

STUDY QUESTIONS

Are there times when you have felt unsure and afraid because of circumstances in your life? Read Genesis 9:1-17. How does the covenant God made with Noah relate to you?

_____

_____

_____

_____

How does that covenant comfort you in a time when the odds seem to be against you?

_____

_____

_____

_____

Have you ever gone through a storm in your life only to get to the end and see a rainbow? Describe that situation below and write a prayer to God thanking Him for the rainbows of life.

_____

_____

_____

_____

CHAPTER 7

GOD FOLLOWS THROUGH

He wiped out every living thing that was on the surface of the ground, from mankind to livestock, to creatures that crawl, to the birds of the sky, and they were wiped off the earth. Only Noah was left, and those that were with him in the ark.
—Gen. 7:23 HCSB

I WILL CONFESS to you that one of the biggest challenges in ministry is the lack of following through on decisions made for the Lord Jesus Christ. Many things start well and with great intention, but many of these things are seldom finished. We are a distracted people. So much is going on all at the same time often causing us to be pulled away from finishing a task properly and completely. I too find follow through personally challenging. Perhaps it is just the way I am wired. It is my personality. I tend to respond far more to facts and less to detail. I love spontaneity and get sidetracked with more interesting things that come along. My home serves as a great illustration. My wife is a wonderful homemaker. I love the way she has always turned our homes into the most beautiful places to live. Our living room is beautifully decorated and everything is in place. However, my study does not keep pace with the rest of the house. That room is my responsibility. I do all of my sermon preparation, writing, and studying in that room. It is my closet. I spend endless hours in my study and most of the time, I have to confess; it is a mess! I have books of every kind stacked up all over the place. There are papers, fax machines, computer equipment, and various things all over the room. I love it in there, but I struggle to keep it looking as good as the rest of our home.

Once in a while I will turn to my wife and say, "I am having a moment of inspiration…do you know what I am going to do? I am going to clean up my study." She simply smiles and says, "Well, have a good time!" For fifteen minutes I am totally focused. I am getting the job done. I am getting blisters on my hands packing things away and straightening things up. After about fifteen minutes, however, I look at my watch and say, "Oops, it is time for tea! I have got to have a cup of tea!" I begin to rationalize, *You have earned the right. You have absolutely killed yourself for fifteen whole minutes.* So I walk out the door and have myself a jolly good cup of tea! I know I am not alone. We have all been there.

Our Heavenly Father is everywhere, all the time and exclusively involved in the affairs of mankind in every way. He never gets distracted. With apologies to the entire British Empire, God never needs to sit down and have a jolly good cup of tea. The sixth word of encouragement is that "God follows through."

Even at the height of the flood, God's presence, His power, and His direction stayed intact. Everyone was dead except for Noah and his family. God had protected them in the midst of the devastation. God is accurate and on time and He always follows through on what He says. You can depend on it. You can trust His Word to be true to the very end.

God is carrying to completion all He has put in front of you. When the Lord has a plan, He will always follow through. It may not be tomorrow, or the next day, but He will definitely follow through. I am reminded of a particular situation when I was a professor at the New Orleans Seminary. One Friday night we got together with a family for some fun and fellowship. Late in the evening, my friend and I decided to get some good junk food at a local grocery store for our families to enjoy. As we were standing in line to pay for our food, I noticed a couple standing in the check-out line next to us. The woman was holding a little girl who looked to be about two years old. The man was standing beside them clutching some change in one hand and a small carton of milk and white powdered donuts in the other. The couple stood staring at the floor and the little girl was quiet and still, unlike any two year old I had ever seen. As I looked at them, trying not to be obvious, God deeply touched my heart. Through my subtle glances, I saw the hopeless, sad looks on their faces. I could not keep my eyes off them.

As we made our purchase and left the store, God impressed my heart to go back into the store and give the man all the money left in my pocket. I told my friend the plan and he quickly concurred and added to the pool of money. Together we had about $200. I rolled it up and walked back into the store right up behind the man. In my South African accent, I told him that I had a gift for him as I slid the money into his hand. I quickly explained that my friend and I were giving him the money because we loved God. We encouraged him to find someone who could tell him about Jesus. I left as quickly as I came and soon forgot all about them.

I do not tell you that story for any praise or accolades on my part. God directed; I merely obeyed, and ten years later I was surprised to learn that God followed through on His plan for that man's life. Early in the new semester I was asked to preach in chapel. After chapel was finished, it was customary for students, professors, and others in attendance to stand in line and shake hands and offer sentiments to the one who had preached. That day I noticed a well-dressed gentleman standing to the side waiting anxiously to speak with me. When all others had greeted me and left, the man approached with his hand outstretched. He said, "Dr. Wilton, I have to share my story with you." I was stunned at what he related.

"Ten years ago, I had no job, no money, no food, no home, and no hope. My wife and I saw no way out of the situation we were in and so we made a suicide pact. We had a two-year-old daughter who was starving and sickly because I could not provide for her. Our plan was to drive to New Orleans and jump off a bridge or tall building to end our lives and pain, taking our daughter with us. My wife could not bear the thought of our daughter dying hungry so we scrounged some change and went to a grocery store very close to this seminary to buy a small carton of milk and some powdered donuts. We were standing in line to buy what we thought would be our daughter's last meal when a man walked up behind me, thrust a roll of money into my hand, and told me to find someone who could tell me about Jesus. Before I could even turn around, he was gone! When I looked down, I was holding $200! I have to tell you, that rocked my world. My wife and I sat in the parking lot of that store all night trying to decide what to do.

"The next morning, with a full tank of gas, we headed back to the tri-cities area of Alabama where we had come from. I found a job at a grocery store and slowly our lives started coming back together.

"Some weeks later, my wife, daughter, and I heard some gospel music as we strolled past a small church. It was like a magnet to me! We went inside, sat on the back row, and as the preacher talked about love and forgiveness of God through the

Lord Jesus Christ, I remembered what that man had said to me in the grocery store in New Orleans. Dr. Wilton, I gave my heart to the Lord Jesus Christ and today is my first day of classes at this seminary! God has called me to preach the gospel. I have wondered about that man for ten years. Today when you were preaching in chapel, I recognized your voice and I knew that man was you."

When the odds were terribly against this man, God stepped in and directed two Christian friends to pool their money, and God followed through with His plan for this man's life.

God directs, we obey, and then the Almighty follows through with His plans, never sleeping, never slumbering. He is always watching out for us, never getting sidetracked and never forgetting. God followed through on His promise to destroy the wicked people of the earth, and He followed through on His promise to take care of Noah, his family, and the animals. Noah simply trusted God and obeyed Him. You will find as you obey Him and trust Him with your life that He is worthy of your trust. Your obedience will not only affect your life but can make an eternal difference in the lives of others.

STUDY QUESTIONS

It is time to read back through the account of Noah in your Bible. Name the ways that God followed through on His promises.

_____

_____

_____

_____

Think of times when you have made promises to God. Did you always follow through?

_____

_____

_____

_____

How does the account of God's faithfulness help you in your times of doubt and fear? Do the odds really matter when God is on your side?

_____

_____

_____

_____

Write a prayer to God asking Him to show you exactly what you need to follow through on today in order to be obedient to Him.

_____

_____

_____

_____

CHAPTER 8

GOD REMEMBERS

God remembered Noah and every living thing, and all the wild animals and the livestock that were with him in the ark.
—Gen. 8:1

FORGETTING IS A normal part of being human. We all forget, and this is true even with regard to things that are very important to us. Some obvious examples include wedding anniversaries, birthdays, and various other special events in our lives. I remember that on one occasion my wife and I drove separate cars to church. Our daughter, who was just a child at the time, drove to church with her mother. When we arrived home, we found that neither one of us had picked her up after the service. We had left our precious little Tweety at church. I had forgotten that it was my duty that day to pick her up, and I simply walked right out of the church, got into my car, and drove home. Well, let me tell you, that was a mistake I never made again. I had some tall apologizing to do when I finally arrived and my little Tweety was standing there with her little lip rolled down and tears streaming down her face. I had to promise ice cream, candy, and a trip to the park to make up for my blunder. When you think about it, what I did was a human sort of thing to do. Often our minds are distracted because we are human and we cannot remember everything.

That is the difference between creation and the Creator. He is fully God and never forgets. The seventh word of encouragement in our study is that "God remembers." God remembered Noah and God remembers you, even when you do not think it is possible.

Think about Job in the Old Testament. Can you imagine all of those calamities coming upon Job? Do you think Job ever thought that God had forgotten him? And so it is with Noah. Do you think there was an instant of time when Noah thought God had forgotten him as well? How easy to come to the conclusion that we actually believe God has forgotten us when we are in the middle of a storm. When the world says the odds are against us, we think it means God has forgotten.

We often forget important things, but God never forgets. We simply cannot fully comprehend that deep truth because we are human. In the midst of busy schedules, we become tired and forgetful. We forget for all kinds of reasons, but mainly because we are human. Our minds are very complex, and often information is stored deep in our brains where we simply cannot pull up the information we need. Not so with God. He remembers every detail of every situation.

When we come to God with our petitions, problems, and struggles, He always remembers. In fact, He already knows about them before we even come to Him in prayer. God does not need to be reminded. So why do we remind him? Why do we bother to pray if He already knows? We bother because He is our Heavenly Father who longs to have a relationship with each of us. He longs to give us the things we need. He wants us to understand who He is and what He can do for us. For example, my wife loves me and I love her, and we both know that very well. I do not need for my wife to tell me she loves me. We both know this and we do not need to be told we are loved. So why do we bother saying, "I love you," to each other? We communicate because we desire to have a relationship with one another.

As our children grow up, we have to teach them many things. We communicate with them constantly to teach them how to live their lives. We also communicate with them because we want a relationship with them and we want them to know how much we love them. Looking back, I remember just how much our kids, like all kids, loved ice cream. We knew they wanted it almost anytime or anywhere. Sometimes we would surprise them, but often they would ask for it. Did we already know they would want ice cream? Of course. But when they asked for it and we could give them what they asked for, it gave us a sense of satisfaction that we had given them something they really desired. And then there is the issue of gratitude. We assumed they were thankful. We knew their track record. We had not raised ungrateful kids. But if they never said "thank you" to us, some of the relationship would be missing. That is why parents teach their children to say thank you.

Having an attitude of gratitude is very important. And we have so much for which to thank our Savior. So, how do we teach our children these things? First, we model it for them. Adults saying "thank you" in front of children is the greatest teaching technique of all. Alternatively, we might also ask that grand old searching-for-something question, "And what are you supposed to say?" Of course we are looking for the "thank you" answer. If they do not say thank you, a parent might say, "Okay, if you cannot say thank you, I will just take your ice cream back." At that point, the child will immediately say, "thank you," because they want to keep their ice cream. So they learn through this process of communication and relationship to be thankful. Why do we go through this process? Have we forgotten that our children like ice cream? Have we forgotten they are thankful? Absolutely not, we want a relationship with them and we want to teach them through that relationship. We simply do not want our children growing up and becoming ingrates. Rather, we want them to learn how to become responsible, caring adults.

God has the same desire for us. He remembers every detail about our lives. He simply wants to have a relationship with us and teach us through that relationship. Often we get confused about that concept, thinking that because God remembers everything He does not need to hear from us. Do not mix those two issues. If you strut through life getting everything and never saying thank you, you will not be able to accomplish God's purpose in your life. Remember the story of the lepers found in Luke 17:11-19? Only one came back to thank Jesus for healing him.

God remembers everything about you and your life. He does not forget even though you may be facing the worst of problems, persecution, illness, or trouble. He still wants to hear from you. He still desires a relationship with you. He wants to communicate His love and He wants to hear of your love for Him. He will teach you how to live through your relationship with Him.

STUDY QUESTIONS

Think about your relationship with God. What do you need to do to improve it?

_____

_____

_____

_____

Just when you are at the end of your rope, and you feel like giving up, God will step in and give you encouragement if you will ask. Do not give up. God has a plan for your life. He is there waiting for you to come to Him, and He wants to help you. He desires a relationship with you. Write a prayer to God asking Him to intervene in your situation right now. Ask for His will to be done and give you the grace to trust Him.

_____

_____

_____

_____

Name a time when you know that God has looked down and remembered you in a time of need.

_____

_____

_____

Write a prayer thanking God for remembering you when you needed Him the most.

_____

_____

_____

_____

GOD EXPECTS

Then Noah built an altar to the Lord, and taking some of all the clean animals and clean birds, he sacrificed burnt offerings on it. The Lord smelled the pleasing aroma and said in his heart: Never again will I curse the ground because of man even though every inclination of his heart is evil from childhood. And never again will I destroy all living creatures, as I have done. As long as the earth endures, seedtime and harvest, cold and heat, summer and winter, day and night will never cease.
—Gen. 8:20-22

EVERY SUMMER I travel with the Mirror Image Youth Choir from our church. We travel long distances to sing and minister, mostly in juvenile detention centers to young men and women who have made bad choices in their lives. It is sad to say, but it is easy to tell which young people will more than likely spend the rest of their lives in prison. They are the ones who heckle, show disrespect, and make obscene gestures to our young people. On the other hand, there are those who are thankful we have come. As those young people walk single file back to their cells, hands behind their backs, in their orange jumpsuits, many of them mouth the words, "Thank you." Often, I have the opportunity to talk personally with some of the young inmates. Many of them will be transferred to adult facilities when they turn eighteen. Although some will get out of these juvenile facilities and then return within six months, others have learned how to be thankful for their difficult experience and will change their actions. They have learned that obedience pays.

Noah listened to God and obeyed Him, and in return God blessed Noah by saving his life, by saving his family, and giving them all a new start. As a result, Noah built an altar to the Lord and sacrificed burnt offerings on it. Did God instruct him to build an altar? If He did, it is not mentioned in Scripture. Keep in mind that God did all of this for Noah. He directed Noah and gave him all of the details. But God expects us to build an altar without being reminded. Noah's altar is our attitude of gratitude. The eighth word of encouragement is that "God expects." He expects us to build an altar. In other words, He expects worship and gratitude for the blessings He gives us. We can be encouraged because this helps us to be who God wants us to be. God expects this from us.

What does it mean to build an altar? It means we are willing to do whatever it takes to let God know what we think of Him. While Noah built one of stone, we build ours of an obedient heart. Ours is an altar of servant-hood. It is our willingness, not only to acknowledge God's goodness and grace towards us, but to respond with a grateful heart. It is our resolve to be faithful to Him in service, in giving and in practical action. God expects something back from us in return for His favor. Too many Christians believe God's direction is a free ride. Every time you do not build an altar to God in response to what He has done for you, you are telling God that you do not think very much of Him. He expects us to follow through with our side of the bargain. God's mercy and grace are available because He is rich in mercy and grace. He does for me what He does because He is God. He is not dependent on me to do what He does, because He is God. He is my Heavenly Father and like every good father, He expects me to do my part.

Have you ever made a deal with God? I have talked with numerous people who were seriously ill, in serious marital trouble, or in some kind of trouble with the law who have said, "God, if You will help me out of this situation, I will start living a life of faith for You." In turn, God worked a miracle in that person's life, and for a few weeks there was an obvious change. Yet, slowly, their enthusiasm dwindled and before long they had forgotten their promise to God and were living the same lifestyle as before. Essentially, they built an altar but never lit the fire!

Has God delivered you? Has He set you free? The Father expects you to build that altar, to go back to the place of your first commitment, to give that gift, to offer that blessing, to travel the distance, to give of your life. God expects for you to build an altar and to light the fire. Your sacrifice will be a sweet aroma in His nostrils.

STUDY QUESTIONS

Have you ever made a deal with God? Write about the promises you made to God during a difficult time in your life.

_____

_____

_____

_____

How did you follow through on those promises?

_____

_____

_____

_____

If you did not follow through on your promises, write a prayer to God telling Him how you feel at this point in your life.

_____

_____

_____

_____

Has God brought you through difficult times? Do you need to "build an altar" to Him, thanking Him for all that has been done for you? Write your thoughts below.

_____

_____

_____

_____

CHAPTER 10

GOD BLESSES

When the Lord smelled the pleasing aroma, He said to Himself, "I will never again curse the ground because of man, even though man's inclination is evil from his youth. And I will never again strike down every living thing as I have done."

—Gen. 8:21 HCSB

God blessed Noah and his sons and said to them, "Be fruitful and multiply and fill the earth."

—Gen. 9:1 HCSB

ON THE MORNING of September 11, 2001, as the twin towers were crashing to the ground in New York City, Jack and Christina Cleland's world was crashing in around them in Spartanburg, South Carolina. This godly young couple loved each other deeply and wanted very much to have a child of their own. They soon found their dream would come true, but a few months into the pregnancy, the doctors gave them devastating news. Their precious baby girl had a genetic disorder that prevented her bone growth. The end result would be death a few hours after she was born. No questions. No remedy. The odds were stacked against them and death would be her fate. Christina would carry this precious child to term and deliver her in the normal fashion. They would hold her, love her, and then soon she would die as they held her.

For more than half of Christina's pregnancy they dealt with the grief of knowing that their precious baby girl, whom they would name Grace, would go to be with Jesus soon after she was born. Somewhere in the back of their minds, they held on to a glimmer of hope that Grace would live and that they would not suffer the loss of their precious little one. But just as the doctors predicted, baby Grace was born on September 11, 2001, and she died five hours later. Jack and Christina grieved the loss of their daughter as any parents would. Their trust in the Lord remained strong and they continued to live in obedience to Him. In the aftermath of their storm, they looked to Him for grace and peace.

One year later, Jack and Christina tried to get pregnant again. A few months later, Christina learned that God was going to bless them with another child. Only this time He doubled their blessings. Nine months later Jackson and Wilson Cleland, their identical twin sons, were born healthy and strong.

A few months after the twins were born, Jack made the announcement that God had called him to go to medical school to be a pediatrician. Jack and Christina moved to the Medical University of South Carolina and began their journey.

Jack and Christina have come full circle in their storm and God has called this young couple to minister to others through the blessing of Grace He sent into their lives. With their fourth child, another healthy son, Andrew, Doctor Jack and Christina serve the Lord in Spartanburg and are deeply loved by all who know them.

Simply put, God blessed Jack and Christina the same way He blessed Noah. The ninth word of encouragement is that "God blesses." The word *blessed* is the same word we use for happiness. It is the word used in the Sermon on the Mount, "*Blessed* are those who are righteous." Being happy is not a shallow thing, like walking around with a smile on one's face. God is referring to the quality of our hearts. To be blessed of God means that we are complete in Him and that we are fulfilled in Him. We have been made whole because of Him.

God loves you. Your circumstances may not always be exactly what you would want. You will face struggles and hard times in your life, but God will walk through the valley with you. He will put His loving arms around you and carry you through the storms that arise. In the aftermath of the storm, you can depend on Him as did Noah. He will keep His promises. With His strength, you can rebuild your life after a divorce. You can gain your strength back after cancer. You can mend that relationship with a wayward child. You can find a fulfilling career after losing a lifelong job. You can recover from the devastation of a natural disaster. You can rebuild your life after losing a loved one.

God has proven His record numerous time in human history. He brought Noah through the storm and blessed him. He brought the children of Israel to the Promised Land and gave them many blessings. He brought Joseph from the pit to the palace. He blessed Job's life in the latter part more than the former part. He brought Jack and Christina Cleland through the devastating loss of a precious child. God has followed through on His promises and has proven His faithfulness throughout the annals of time. And he will prove His faithfulness in your life as well. You can trust the Lord, because the final word of encouragement is the eternal truth that God is at work.

STUDY QUESTIONS

Write about a time in your life when you went through a storm, but in the end were blessed by God.

_____

_____

_____

_____

Name the blessings you can think of that are in your life right now.

_____

_____

_____

_____

Stop and think about the many blessings in your life, and then write a prayer thanking the Almighty for what you have and what He has done.

_____

_____

_____

_____

GOD WORKS

And we know that in all things God works for the good of those that love Him, to those that have been called according to His purpose.

—Rom. 8:28

GOD IS SOVEREIGN! He is in control even when the world insinuates the odds are against you. He is constantly working all things together for the good of those who love Him. The tenth word of encouragement is that "God works." That is a promise, and He never breaks a promise! He has always been at work, and He is still at work today. In fact, there is never a time when God is not working.

Often we misunderstand this idea. God does not cause all things to happen, but He works for the good of those who love Him in those things. Often bad things happen as a result of sin in our lives. For example, a teenage girl is killed in a car accident as a result of drinking alcohol, using cocaine, and then driving under the influence. A terrible thing happened because that young person chose to drink, use cocaine, and drive. Did God cause that? No, but He can work all of those things together for the good of those who love Him. He can work good in the lives of that young person's parents, siblings, friends, and even people who barely knew her. He can use this disaster as an example to perhaps bring about change in her family. He can cause other parents to step up and value their children more as a result of this tragedy. He can cause other young people to realize their lives are fragile and they need to accept Christ as their Savior. He can work all of these things for good.

On the other hand, sometimes bad things happen as a result of another person's sin, such as a young person being killed in a car accident because another person was drinking and driving. Did God cause this? No, but He can work all of these things together for the good of those who love Him.

Often bad things happen simply because we live in a fallen world. God can do anything He wants, but often He is blamed for things He had nothing to do with, except for the fact that He will work in that situation for our good if we will allow Him. Nevertheless, God is sovereign and in control of all things, and He will never allow something to happen that will not work for our good at some point.

God worked all things together for good in the life of Noah before, during, and after the flood. And it is the same with us. Since the day we were conceived, God has been at work in all the circumstances of our lives for our good. This is not because we deserve it or because we have earned it. It is simply because He loves us. The most difficult time to understand God's love is when we are hurting and do not know which road to take. Even then, God is at work and Scripture tells us He is working for our good. Let's dissect Romans 8:28 and consider what it really means for us today.

WE KNOW

If we love the Lord, we know. That is a tremendous confirmation. I love the phrase "You've just got to believe." I'm a diehard New Orleans Saints football fan. If you do not know about the Saints, they have adopted a slogan. If you go to a Saints football game you will see signs everywhere that say, "I Believe!" What do they believe? For years and years the roar of the crowd was not enough to propel them to championship status. I was even a fan during the "Aints" days but still loved watching Archie Manning when he played in the 70s and early 80s. Guess what? Along came Drew Brees and a team with all the "I Believe" one can imagine. And it happened. Super Bowl champs of the 2009 season.

As Christians, God's Word tells us to believe, but the basis of that belief is an absolute confidence that God has saved us through the shed blood of Jesus Christ. If you know that salvation is secure, you can also know that what salvation brings is secure. When one comes to Christ, it is not simply a matter of receiving forgiveness and hope. It is that God's salvation is accompanied by all the resources necessary for you to go through the journey of life.

THAT GOD

God is the Alpha and Omega, the first and the last, the beginning and the end! God is God. He is the guarantor. He is the signature signed to every check that has been deposited by the Holy Spirit on behalf of you and me. If we love God, we know "that God."

IS AT WORK

This means God is gainfully engaged. He is actively employed in human affairs, and persistently interested in everything about you and me. You may feel like God has abandoned you, but you cannot always trust your feelings. You cannot always follow your heart. The Bible says in Jeremiah 17:9, "The heart is deceitful above all things and beyond cure. Who can understand it?" So we see that we must trust God's Word and not our hearts and emotions. Scripture assures us that the Father is always at work in our lives.

CAUSING ALL THINGS TO WORK TOGETHER

I love to think about this. The Greek word used for "all things together" is the word *synergos*. The word synergy or synergism is derived from this word. It means "working together," or, "all things coming together in one purpose." Think about a cheerleading squad as they train for harmony and oneness. Each cheerleader is supposed to do the same thing at the same time in the same rhythm. When this happens we see a great picture of synergy. Everyone working together for one purpose is a beautiful picture. It is the same with life. Say you are experiencing a bad situation, then a good situation, then a bump in the road, and later on a hardship, a struggle, a joy, and a time of peace. God synergizes all of these things and brings them together to dance in rhythm! He makes music out of our lives. He combines the instruments of the orchestra into a harmony of sound that spirals into the heavens. God causes all things to work together. This may be hard to comprehend when you are in the valley, but hold on, trust God, and you will see.

FOR THE GOOD

"For the good" means that God has our interest at heart. But keep in mind that our definition of good differs from God's definition. It is God's measurement, not ours. God can cause righteousness to work for our good. What part of righteousness can God bring to bear on me to make good for me? His goodness, mercy, love, grace, and all the other attributes of God's character can be brought to bear. And His faithfulness can be brought to bear on my life's circumstances. He can bring things into my life to produce good according to His standard by funneling all the good things that happen in my life through His character. In this way more is possible through Christ than I could ever imagine. And not only will God use good for good, but He will also use evil for good. Let me use two illustrations of evil in our lives, suffering and temptation.

Suffering

Suffering is bad. It is hurtful and painful. When we are in the middle of suffering it is difficult to ever see that good could come from it. So, why was James able to say "Consider it pure joy, my brothers and sisters, whenever you face trials of many kinds." Was he serious? What was his foundation for saying that, and what was he trying to say? Do you remember Moses? Moses chose to suffer affliction with the people of God rather than enjoy the pleasures of sin for a season. And, what did it produce? It produced the mighty act of God. He aligned himself in suffering in order to produce what God was working to bring about, and the children of Israel were led out of bondage.

How can God use our suffering? One way is for suffering to cause us to hate sin and become more faithful. Suffering can cause us to reevaluate our priorities. We need a constant reevaluation of our priorities and what we do with the stuff of our lives: our investments, where our money is going, what we are doing with our time, where our energy is, where our affections are set. God can and does allow suffering to come upon some people to work that together for the good of that one for whom He has a specific plan and purpose. It is certainly hard to understand, but God is at work in all things.

Temptation

Temptation is not good, either. The Bible says God will never tempt us, that only the devil can do that. Jesus was tempted. Can the Father use something as evil as temptation and somehow turn it into good? The answer is yes because very often God uses evil to drive us to our knees. Temptation can humble our attitude and smash our pride. God allows temptation to occur in our lives just to get us where he wants us to be. The Creator is at work, causing all things to work together for the good.

OF THOSE THAT LOVE GOD

It is easy to love God after going through the storms of life and seeing Him work. During the storm it is harder to find that love and trust in your heart. As Noah rode out the storm and took care of the animals, I am sure he had to continually remind himself that God had made a promise. He had to keep God's words continually in his mind. When you are going through the storms of life, keep His words continually in your own mind. Meditate on the verses that reveal God's promises to you. Trust Him, and in the end you, as Noah, will see the rainbow. Love Him with all of your heart. Do not blame Him, trust Him. Do not become bitter and soon you will become better!

WHO HAVE BEEN CALLED ACCORDING TO HIS PURPOSE

God works all things together for those who love him and have been called according to His purpose. How is one called according to God's purpose? This happens when you give your heart to the Lord. Give your life to Christ today if you have not done so in the past. This is not about feeling good. This is about the foundation we have in the Lord Jesus Christ. In Christ, more is possible—far more than you and I could ever imagine because

Jesus makes the difference. When you love God, when you know you belong to Him, all of a sudden you begin interpreting everything that happens to you through God's eyes. The world may say the odds are against you, or you may find yourself in a deep trough, or you may find yourself on a mountain top, but your whole understanding takes on a different meaning when you understand this precept of God's Word.

As we close this book of encouragement on defying the odds, remember that God is who He says He is. God is God, and He is in control, with you in the palm of His hand. God!

- He sees your struggle.
- He grieves with you when your heart is broken.
- He knows your name and is calling you to Himself.
- He will direct your path and set your feet on solid ground.
- He has established His covenant with you and has a purpose for your life. He wants to use your circumstances for His Kingdom plan. He never wastes anything that happens to you, and will use your circumstances to bring you to the place in your life He wants you to be.
- He always follows through. He will never leave you nor forsake you.
- He remembers you in the middle of the storm. He never forgets.
- He expects a response from you. He expects you to be thankful and respond to His love.
- He blesses you in the end and restores your life in ways that you could never imagine.
- He is always working in all things for your good!

If you find yourself in a situation where the world tells you the odds are stacked against you, do not to give up. Trust God and obey Him on a daily basis. Gaze at God and glance at your circumstances. Often people gaze at the circumstances and glance at God, but no one finds the answer to life's problem by gazing at the problem itself. You will only find that answer when you fix your eyes on God and Scripture. Pray for heaven's will to be done in your life and Christ will see you through to the end. He is working all around you and He has a perfect plan for your life. Rest in His love as He synergizes all of these things and brings them together to dance in rhythm! Allow Him to make a beautiful symphony of your life as He works all things together for your good. Trust Him today and see what He will do.

STUDY QUESTIONS

Take a few moments to stop and think about the good things that have happened in your life. Write some of them below.

_____

_____

_____

_____

Now, think about the bad things that have happened throughout your life and write them below.

_____

_____

_____

_____

Write a prayer below asking God to show you how He is working all of those things together for your good.

_____

_____

_____

_____

Continue your prayer by writing about your love for God. If you have never asked Jesus Christ to come into your life, write a prayer asking Him to take control of your life and deliver you from sin.

_____

_____

_____

_____

Think about your life as a whole. Write the ways you see that God has worked those things together for your good.

_____

_____

_____

_____

HAS THE ENCOURAGING WORD IMPACTED YOUR LIFE FOR JESUS CHRIST?

SHARE YOUR TESTIMONY WITH US!

"LET US ENCOURAGE ONE ANOTHER..."
HEBREWS 10:25

866-899-WORD (9673)
THE ENCOURAGING WORD
P.O. BOX 2110
SPARTANBURG, SC 29304

WWW.THEENCOURAGINGWORD.ORG

WITH DR. DON WILTON

The Encouraging Word with Dr. Don Wilton is a non-profit national broadcast ministy dedicated to spreading the Gospel of Jesus Christ throughout the world and connecting people to strong churches in their own communities.

To learn more about The Encouraging Word and available ministry resources, including other books and sermons by Dr. Don Wilton...

Please visit
www.TheEncouragingWord.org

or contact

The Encouraging Word, Inc.
P. O. Box 2110
Spartanburg, SC 29304
1-866-899-WORD (9673)